THE RED AND THE BLACK

Borgo Press Books by FRANK J. MORLOCK

Chuzzlewit: A Play in Two Acts
Falstaff: A Play in Four Acts (with William Shakespeare, John Dennis, and William Kendrick)
Outrageous Women: Lady Macbeth and Other French Plays (editor and translator)
The Red and the Black: A Play in Three Acts (adapted from the novel by Stendhal)
The Stendhal Hamlet Scenarios and Other Shakespearean Shorts from the French (editor and translator)

THE RED AND THE BLACK

A PLAY IN THREE ACTS

FRANK J. MORLOCK

Adapted from the Novel by Stendhal

THE BORGO PRESS
MMXII

THE RED AND THE BLACK

Copyright © 2012 by Frank J. Morlock

FIRST EDITION

Published by Wildside Press LLC

www.wildsidebooks.com

DEDICATION

For Robert Haas,

for many years of friendship

CONTENTS

CAST OF CHARACTERS	9
ACT I, Scene 1	11
ACT I, Scene 2	15
ACT I, Scene 3	25
ACT I, Scene 4	35
ACT II, Scene 5	53
ACT II, Scene 6	67
ACT II, Scene 7	83
ACT III, Scene 8	113
ACT III, Scene 9	137
ABOUT THE AUTHOR	153

CAST OF CHARACTERS

Young Julien
The Bishop
Julien
Sorel
A Servant
Monsieur Reynal
Madame Reynal (Louise)
Alphonse
Fouqué
Father Pirard
Marquis de la Mole
Mathilde
Count Norbert
First Gent
Second Gent
Several Masks
Monsieur de Croisenois (not a speaking part)
Count Altamira
Prince Araceli (not a speaking part)
Reactionary Gentleman
Jailer
Priest

ACT I
SCENE 1

The apartment of the Bishop.

A young man in priestly attire is practicing benedictions before a mirror.

The Young Julien enters, trembling, carrying a miter.

Julien (to himself)

It is my duty to speak. (he advances, the Bishop turns)

Bishop

Well, Monsieur, is it ready yet?

Julien

Yes, Excellency.

Bishop

I need it immediately. (he places it on) There, it will

stay. (he adjusts it, steps aside a little, practices several more benedictions) What do you think, Monsieur Julien? Does it look right?

Julien

Perfect, Excellency.

Bishop

Too far back, perhaps? That would look silly. But, it mustn't fall over the eyes like a visor either.

Julien

I think it's very good.

Bishop

The King is used to venerable clergymen. I mustn't look frivolous because of my age.

Julien

To be a Bishop, and so young. How clever you must be.

Bishop

It isn't age that makes a servant of God. (pause) The King is here to pay his respects to a relic. But make no mistake, he is here to pay his respects to us...the clergy. Never forget, Julien, that you are about to see one of the greatest kings on earth on his knees before the servants of God. These servants are weak, persecuted, martyred in this world, but triumphant in Heaven—and, if we are careful, here on Earth as well.

Julien

On Earth as it is in Heaven.

(Julien crosses himself, awestruck, as the curtain descends.)

CURTAIN

ACT I
SCENE 2

Some years later.

Monsieur Reynal's garden.

Julien and his father, Sorel, enter.

Sorel (to a servant)

We are here to see the mayor. (the servant hesitates) On his invitation...on business.

Servant

Please wait. I'll inform Monsieur Reynal.

(The servant enters the house.)

Sorel (collaring his son)

Answer me without lying, if you can, Bookworm. How did you get to know his wife? When did you speak to her?

Julien

I don't know her. I've only seen her at Church.

Sorel

Ah, but you must have stared at her, didn't you? Scum.

Julien

Never. I only see God when I'm in Church. (there is just a shade, only a shade of insincerity in this protest)

Sorel

Does God wear petticoats? (pause) There's something behind this. Why should the mayor choose you as a tutor for his children? But, I'll never find out from you, you crafty little sneak.

Julien

I'd still like to know what I'm going to get for it.

Sorel

Board, lodging, clothing, plus three hundred a year. Isn't that enough for you, my fine gentleman?

Julien

I won't be a servant.

Sorel

Who said that, you idiot? You think I'd let my son be a servant?

Julien

I won't eat with the servants.

Sorel

Shut up and leave this to me, you greedy little bastard.

Julien

I'll die before I'll eat with the servants.

(Madame and Monsieur Reynal enter from the house. Reynal is much older than his pretty wife.)

Reynal (to his wife)

Let him boast about his carriage. He doesn't have a tutor for his children.

Madame Reynal

Perhaps he'll steal this one from us.

Reynal

Then you approve of my plans? All right, then, it's

settled.

Madame Reynal (slyly)

Good Heavens, dear, how quickly you make up your mind.

Reynal

Strength of character. It's going to cost us, but we must maintain our position. (approaching Sorel) Welcome to my house, Monsieur Sorel. This is your son Julien? Charmed I'm sure. (Julien makes an awkward bow, but stands mute) Your father has told you of the arrangements made for you? (Julien tries to speak but words fail him, he contents himself with a murderous look) Monsieur Sorel, this is Madame de Reynal, my wife.

Sorel

Enchanted.

Reynal (to his wife)

Why don't you discuss your orders with our young tutor, while I arrange matters with his father.

(Julien and Madame Reynal withdraw to the other end of the garden.)

Reynal

Everything is settled satisfactorily?

Sorel (churlishly)

Nothing is settled.

(Reynal and Sorel mime a ferocious argument.)

Madame Reynal

Do you mean to say you know Latin, Monsieur?

Julien (defensive, ironic)

That is why I've come as a tutor, Madame!

Madame Reynal

You won't beat the children?

Julien

Beat them? Why should I do that?

Madame Reynal

You will promise me to be kind to them, not to scold them?

Julien (struck by her beauty at last)

I'll obey you in everything.

Madame Reynal

How old are you, Monsieur?

Julien

Nineteen.

Madame Reynal

My eldest son is eleven. You can reason with him. His father slapped him once and I was sick for a week.

Julien

I swear, before God, I will never beat your children.

Madame Reynal

What's your name, Monsieur?

Julien (struggling to get it out)

Julien Sorel. I'm very nervous about entering a strange house. I crave your protection. I hope you will forgive my many mistakes.

(Madame Reynal and Julien continue their conversation in mime.)

Sorel

If I take him back, he will keep this coat you promised to give him?

Reynal

Of course.

Sorel

Now, about the money.

Reynal

You know my offer. You accepted yesterday.

Sorel

That's true, I don't deny it. But, we are poor. (with a stroke of genius) Today, we've had a better one.

Reynal

So. May I ask from whom?

Sorel

No matter. Not only is the money better, but my son will eat with the family.

Reynal

He shall do that here as well. And I add a hundred to my offer. Is it agreed?

Sorel

Agreed. (reluctant still)

Reynal

Well, your father and I are agreed, young man. Everyone will treat you with respect here. If I am satisfied with you, I will help you establish yourself later on. (Reynal takes Julien by the arm) Now, there are some things you must understand immediately. I don't want to see either your family or your friends here. I shall give you an advance on your salary, but on your word of honor, you must not give one sou to your father.

Julien

That's easily given.

Reynal

Everyone here is to call you Monsieur. Alphonse. (a servant appears) Take Monsieur Sorel's luggage to his room. (the servant takes the traps) And now, it is time for you to meet the children. A little dignity will not be amiss. I want them to respect you.

Julien

Thank you, Monsieur.

(Julien leaves to join Madame Reynal.)

Reynal (addressing old Sorel)

Our business is at an end, Monsieur.

Sorel

Good day.

(Madame Reynal returns.)

Reynal

Without bowing. What a churl. (noticing his wife) Well, what do you think of our new acquisition, my dear?

Madame Reynal

I'm not so pleased with that upstart peasant as you are. You'll make him insolent with your kindness. I know the type. We'll have to get rid of him in a month.

Reynal

So be it. But, people will have gotten used to seeing

our children with a tutor. And, we'll get another one. After all, educated peasants are a dime a dozen. So much the better.

CURTAIN

ACT I
SCENE 3

Fouqué's humble lodgings.

Fouqué

Julien, so good to see you.

Julien

I told you, I don't forget my friends.

Fouqué

This is delightful. In fact, I was going to look you up anyway.

Julien

I beat you to it.

Fouqué

I have a business proposition to put to you, Julien.

Julien

Really? I'm hardly in a position to undertake any business. You sound so serious.

Fouqué

I am serious. I apologize for sounding so pompous. My timber business is going very well, and I need some help, a partner, in fact.

Julien

If I hear of any one....

Fouqué

You, Julien. I want you.

Julien

Me? I'm honored, but I'm soon to take my vows. And, besides that, I've got this tutoring job. I'm not a priest, but I am of a scholarly turn....

Fouqué

With your education, we could make three times what I'm making now....

Julien

Really, I'm touched, but....

Fouqué

You're not cut out to be a priest.

Julien

Everyone seems to think that, except me.

Fouqué

You're ambitious, Julien.

Julien

Who denies it?

Fouqué

And, you've quarreled with Reynal or you wouldn't be here.

Julien

You've a good head on your shoulders for judging people. You'll make your fortune.

Fouqué

Julien, if we become partners we'll be rich in a few

years....

Julien

But, I'd like to keep my tutoring position, just for the present.

Fouqué

Reynal despises you, like the mud on his boots....

Julien

I have certain reasons...I also have to think of my vocation.

Fouqué

If you don't feel like living with me, you can go back to the seminary after a short time. And, I can promise you the best parish in the district, because I supply firewood to the Archbishop and several of the leading citizens who need it for their factories, so....

Julien

I get the parish, because you supply the firewood? (he laughs)

Fouqué

Exactly. You're too proud. It's honest labor.

Julien

You're right. I am too proud. I don't want to be a merchant.

Fouqué

As a merchant, I'll be able to buy and sell you in five years.

Julien

That's true. But a tutor, a priest, has a certain position.

Fouqué

Shit. That may have been true fifty years ago, but not today. Money counts today.

Julien

Not at the highest levels.

Fouqué

Who's talking about the highest levels?

Julien (serious)

I am.

Fouqué

You want to join the aristocracy?

Julien

With all my heart and soul.

Fouqué (whistles)

I always knew you were ambitious. But, that's exactly why you shouldn't be a priest.

Julien

On the contrary, that's exactly why I should become a priest. There are only two roads for a poor man in France. They are the Army and the Clergy. I have chosen the Clergy because since Napoleon, it is clear that the most one can hope for from the Army is to be a General.

Fouqué

The most one can hope to be.... This beats all.

Julien

As you said, I am ambitious. I've never told anyone of my dreams before. I forbid you ever to repeat it.

Fouqué

Who would believe me? Still, a few years with me. You could build a nest egg....

Julien

Why should I throw away a half dozen years of my life? I'd be twenty- eight by then, and at that age Napoleon had already performed his greatest deeds. Who knows, if after obscurely heaping up money selling timber, my soul wouldn't be as coarse as the merchandise.

Fouqué

Napoleon again. If you feel degraded to be a timber merchant, I'll say no more.

Julien

I don't mean it that way. But, surely you can see it's not the timber from which heroes are made.

Fouqué

I suppose so.

Julien

It's not a choice between vice and virtue, but between a prosperous, though mediocre, future and a glorious dream. Perhaps I have no real strength of character or I wouldn't doubt my capacity to work for you for a while and re-emerge as a hero.

Fouqué

Napoleon...heroes...aristocracy? What next? And yet, you put up with Reynal's insults.

Julien

What if I took possession of his wife right under his nose?

Fouqué

And now, a Don Juan!

Julien

I owe it to myself to become her lover.

Fouqué

Think of the risk.

Julien

One must dare. Besides, if I do make a name for myself, and someone jeers at me for having been a tutor, I can say that love drove me to it.

Fouqué

But, what makes you think you'll succeed with her. She's got a reputation for being pretty stuck up.

Julien

Oh, of success, there's no doubt. (nonchalantly) I'll have to tell her I love her.

Fouqué

But, for an inexperienced gauche person like you, to love a great lady.

Julien

I may be inexperienced and crude, but at least I won't be weak.

Fouqué

Julien....

Julien

Yes, and lacking in character, too. I'd have made a bad soldier for Napoleon. But a little intrigue with the lady of the house will keep me amused for a while. I must tell her I lover her at once.

(He leaves, leaving Fouqué stunned.)

CURTAIN

ACT I
SCENE 4

The Reynal garden. Several months later.

Reynal (crumpling a letter and slamming his fist)

He's come here to find fault.

Madame Reynal

But, how can he? You're scrupulously honest in the way you handle the funds allotted to the poor.

Reynal

This little Parisian inspector will publish articles in all the liberal press.

Madame Reynal

You never read them anyway.

Reynal

Others do. How do you prove you're an honest man?

Madame Reynal

Forget him, there's nothing you can do. I want to talk to you about Julien.

Reynal

Is he getting out of line?

Madame Reynal

On the contrary.

Reynal

Let's not lose him. He's getting a reputation now. Damn it, I don't want someone else to have him.

Madame Reynal

I'd like you to give him a little extra, so he can have some presentable clothes made for himself.

Reynal

Let's not give him delusions of grandeur.

Madame Reynal

But, he's done very well, and he refused my offer.

Reynal

What? You tolerated a refusal from a servant?

Madame Reynal

He is not a servant.

Reynal

Anyone not of noble birth who works for you is a servant. Remember that! I'm going to have a talk with this Monsieur Julien.

Madame Reynal

I beg you not to humiliate him.

Reynal

Hey, Monsieur Julien!

Madame Reynal

I WILL NOT HAVE YOU HUMILIATE HIM!

Reynal

He hasn't spent enough time with the children lately.

Hey, MONSIEUR!

Madame Reynal

I won't have this.

Julien (insolent)

Were you calling me?

Reynal

Yes, Monsieur. It seems you have been so impolite as to refuse a gift from my wife. Besides that, you've neglected the children.

Julien (icily)

Monsieur, do you think your children would have made the same progress with any other tutor? If your answer is no, how dare you complain that I neglect them?

Reynal

I didn't say they weren't improving, I merely....

Julien (furious)

As for your wife's kind gift, I refused it because she thought it unnecessary to mention it to you, for fear you would not approve. (to Madame Reynal) I am humble, Madame, but not base. I'd be less than a footman if I put myself in a position of having to hide anything concerning money from Monsieur de Reynal. I am prepared to account for every penny of the money I have received since entering this house.

Reynal

If I had understood your motives...I should not have been angry. You were very correct.

Julien

I can live without you, Monsieur....

Reynal

I didn't mean to upset you.

Julien

That's not enough for me, Monsieur. Think of the infamous things you have said to me. And, in front of your wife, too.

Reynal

Now, now—

Julien

I know where to go when I leave your house, Monsieur.

Reynal (to Madame Reynal)

So, that's it. (to Julien) I apologize. Does that satisfy you? I hope you will accept a raise of a hundred francs without being offended. Are we agreed? Fine. Now, if you will excuse me, I have some business to attend to. (to Madame Reynal) That's another hundred francs you've cost me with your nonsense.

(Reynal goes into the house.)

Madame Reynal

Julien.

Julien

That was your doing.

Madame Reynal

You were magnificent. Don't be angry, dearest. I didn't intend it that way.

Julien

He's just made the greatest apology such a base nature is capable of.

Madame Reynal

You were so heroic.

Julien

I've won a battle. A real battle.

Madame Reynal

He's really under a lot of pressure. Anyway, you can't leave us.

Julien

Why not?

Madame Reynal

What about the children?

Julien

They'll get along. Tutors are a dime a dozen.

Madame Reynal (choking)

And me?

Julien

You could find another lover.

Madame Reynal

Julien!

Julien

One from your own class. One you don't humiliate all the time without meaning to.

Madame Reynal

Do I humiliate you? I love you. It seems to me that I humble myself.

Julien

You love me. But after this moment of weakness for which your pride is reproaching you, you will be just as haughty as ever.

Madame Reynal

Have I been haughty?

Julien

In your eyes, I am not well-born.

Madame Reynal

Julien, I never even considered such a thing! You just say that to hurt me. I think you no longer love me.

I'm ten years older than you. That's it. This is your way of getting rid of me.

Julien

Louise, that's not it at all.

Madame Reynal

Then, why did you lock your door to me last night?

Julien

Because it was too dangerous.

Madame Reynal

It wasn't too dangerous the night before, was it?

Julien

Didn't you order me to be careful?

Madame Reynal

I only meant in public.

Julien

You can still order me if it regards the children. There I am still your servant. But, in responding to my love, you should assume equality. It's impossible to love without equality.

Madame Reynal

But, but, Julien, if my husband had heard anything, I'd have lost—

Julien

Would you regret losing your life?

Madame Reynal

Very much, since I have known you. But if I must, I will. Oh Julien, you aren't tired of me?

Julien

No.

Madame Reynal

If only I'd known you ten years ago, when I could still pass for a pretty woman.

Julien

Stop that.

Madame Reynal

Oh darling, how I hope to live long enough to see you

in all your glory. France needs a great man...

Julien

You're the only person who believes in me.

Madame Reynal

Are you happy? Do you feel I love you enough?

Julien

You know I do.

Madame Reynal

Then, it's not all for nothing. I know I'm damned beyond all redemption. You were young and I seduced you. God will forgive you, but I'm damned.

Julien

Don't talk such nonsense.

Madame Reynal

I know it by a sure sign. God is punishing me now.

Julien

What sign? What are you talking about?

Madame Reynal

Stanislas is sick.

Julien

Just a bad cold.

Madame Reynal

Last night, I dreamed he was dead. God will take him from me for my sin.

Julien

You're simply imagining things.

Madame Reynal

I'm scared, Julien. But, not repentant. I'd do it again no matter what happens. I'm not afraid of Hell. If only He won't take my children from me.

Julien

If you keep working yourself up like this, your husband will. You'll give everything away.

Reynal (entering)

Louise, I think we'd best send for the doctor. His fever is worse.

Madame Reynal (beside herself)

No, listen to me. I want you to know the whole truth. It's I who am killing my son. Heaven is punishing me for my sins.

Reynal

What sins have you ever committed, for goodness sake? The child is not dying. He simply needs a doctor.

Reynal (exiting)

Women! Always calm in a crisis.

Julien

That was close. If you husband was a man of any perception.

Madame Reynal

Go away from me. In the name of God, leave this house: it's your presence that's killing my son. God is punishing me, and He is just. I worship his justice. My crime is horrible, and I was without remorse. I didn't give my baby a thought. All I wanted was for my husband to give you some money. Now my baby is dying....

Julien

You love your son more than you love me?

Madame Reynal

No. Monster that I am, I love you more. Go away.

Julien

No lover could ask for more. I'll leave you, if that will help. But I adore you. But, if I go now, you're sure to tell your husband everything. That automaton will put the whole blame on you.

Madame Reynal

So much the better.

Julien

You'll ruin his life, too.

Madame Reynal

Perhaps throwing myself in the mud will save my son. Perhaps then God will forgive me.

Julien

Better if I punish myself. I'm guilty too. I'll return to the seminary.

Madame Reynal

Ah.

Julien

Perhaps such a sacrifice will appease God.

Madame Reynal (in agony)

I don't want you to go.

Julien

If only I could take his illness on myself.

Madame Reynal (hugging him impulsively)

Oh, you love him, too. I believe you, I believe you. (pushing him away in horror) Oh, why aren't you my baby's father. Then it wouldn't be a sin to love you more than my son.

Julien

Tell me what to do. I no longer matter. I'll obey you no matter what your orders are.

Madame Reynal

I'm not sure I can be silent without you here.

Julien

Do you want me to stay and love you like a brother?

Madame Reynal

And, what about me? Is it in my power to love you that way?

Julien

For the sake of your children, you must promise me to say nothing.

Madame Reynal

I promise.

Julien

I will return to the seminary tonight. We mustn't be together any longer.

Madame Reynal

Julien—

Julien

Yes?

Madame Reynal

Are you doing this for me, or for yourself? Could it be that you have never loved me?

Julien

Louise.

Madame Reynal

No. Don't answer. I don't want to know. I have not just loved you, I have worshipped you. Go. And do not come back and do not write. Somehow I must learn to live without you. Goodbye forever, my darling. (going in, then turns) You must kiss Stanislas goodbye before you go.

Julien (turning toward the audience as she leaves)

How could a simple peasant like myself have inspired love in such a pure heart? That is a heart in which it is glorious to reign. Well, have I played my part well? Have I done everything that I, in duty, owed myself?

CURTAIN

ACT II
SCENE 5

The Seminary.

Fouqué (entering)

At last I managed to get in.

Julien

Fouqué!

Fouqué

I've been here five times, and they wouldn't let me see you. Why don't you manage to get out?

Julien

I'm testing myself.

Fouqué

Now, I suppose you want to be a saint. The Napoleon

of the Heavenly Choir.

Julien

It's good to see a human face.

Fouqué

You don't like it here, then? And you, so learned in theology....

Julien

Learning means nothing here. It counts only in appearance. Could it be that they value it at its true worth?

Fouqué

I've never heard you talk like this before.

Julien

I was foolish enough to be proud because I was top in my class. That only made me enemies. I should do like other clever fellows and contrive to appear stupid.

Fouqué

But, Julien—

Julien

I've spent my life congratulating myself on being different from other men. Being different breeds only hatred.

Fouqué

Then, you no longer desire to be a priest?

Julien

Who knows. Perhaps I'll spend my life selling pews in Heaven to the faithful.

Fouqué

Well, you could sell timber.

Julien

It's probably a nobler profession.

Fouqué

But Julien, I had heard that you were the Prior's favorite.

Julien

Well, I am...of sorts. But, he's the sort who believes in doing nothing for those he loves most. He thinks

God will do it.

Fouqué

Why?

Julien

He places justice higher than love. The more he loves you the less you can expect from him. He would rather die than acknowledge the favoritism he feels. Anyway, he couldn't do me much good, even if he tried.

Fouqué

Why not?

Julien

Because he's a Jansenist, and the Bishop is a Jesuit. Father Pirard's blessing is the kiss of death to any man's ambitions.

Fouqué

Why not quit?

Julien

I abominate this life.

Fouqué

I still need a partner.

Julien

No. I will not allow them to hound me out, the swine. Ah, Fouqué, do you know that in this seminary there are men worthy of being Pope?

Fouqué

Really?

Julien

You bet. They make peasants Popes these days. Sixtus V was a swineherd. Why not genuine swine?

Fouqué

You're too bitter.

Julien (pacing)

By the way, how are my former charges doing?

Fouqué

Growing. But the mother has become extremely pious.

Julien (interested)

Has she?

Fouqué

Of the most exalted kind.

Father Pirard (entering)

Brother Julien, I wish to.... Ah, you are not alone.

Fouqué

I was just leaving, Father. Goodbye, Julien. Remember my offer stands. Be back again. (Fouqué exits)

Julien

I'll think about it. I'll write you.

Father Pirard

Julien, you know I am fond of you.

(Julien takes his hand and kisses it. Pirard, although a man of strong feelings is aghast. He hates all display of emotion.)

Father Pirard

What are you doing? (faltering) Yes, my son, I'm fond

of you. Heaven knows it's against my will. I ought to be just and neither love nor hate. But I am weak. (pause) I see something in you that offends the vulgar. Wherever you go, jealousy and hatred will follow. Hold fast to truth, my son. If you do, God will confound your enemies

Julien

I give you my word of honor.

Father Pirard

That expression is out of place here. It is too suggestive of the vain honor of men of the world.

Julien

I have sinned, Father.

Father Pirard

Julien, I am troubled about you. You are not lacking in either memory or intelligence, or in apparent devotion to the Lord.

Julien

Thank you, Father.

Father Pirard

One question troubles me. Is it sincere?

Julien

But—

Father Pirard

You have a cheerful face, Julien. The faces of this world are truly theatres of falseness. Do not protest. If you have had devotion in the past, you will need much more in the future. I say this to you, because I am about to take a step which will leave you without a protector in this den of wolves.

Julien

I don't understand.

Father Pirard

I am about to resign. I want you to carry my letter of resignation to the Bishop, who will, no doubt, be delighted.

Julien

You're leaving?

Father Pirard

And you will be alone, Julien. Because you were dear to me, you will be a marked man.

Julien

But, where will you go? What will you do?

Father Pirard

I am not entirely without friends. If I had been, I should not have survived as long as I have. The Marquis de la Mole has, for many years, urged me to become his personal secretary.

Julien

The Cabinet Minister? Then, you are truly fortunate.

Father Pirard

Julien, are you firm in your intent to stay here?

Julien

What else can I do?

Father Pirard

You can come with me.

Julien

With you, Father?

Father Pirard

The Marquis is also in need of a private secretary who is not a priest. A man capable of appearing in the world, and who is not unduly troubled in his conscience over fine points of morality.

Julien

This is very unexpected.

Father Pirard

You'll live in the house of the Marquis, who is one of the greatest nobles in France. You'll dress in black, but not like an ecclesiastic. You will compose most of the Marquis' correspondence and run his library.

Julien

But, if I should not be equal to the task?

Father Pirard

With your classical learning, it will be simple. However, if after a year, you haven't proved useful, I have arranged for your return to the seminary.

Julien

But, my vocation....

Father Pirard

You'll pursue theological studies regularly. I'll see to that. Look on this as a test.

Julien

You've thought of everything.

Father Pirard

The main point is that you prove trustworthy. It is possible that persons will offer you enormous advantages...or to be blunt, bribes, just for a peep at the Marquis' letters.

Julien (indignant)

Oh, Monsieur!

Father Pirard

It is strange that, poor as you are, and after several years in a seminary, you are still subject to outbursts of righteous indignation. Well, do you accept?

Julien

What is the Marquis like?

Father Pirard

Proud, but open. He proposes to give you the outrageous sum of a hundred crowns to start. I could not dissuade him. He is used to having his own way. He is capricious. He'll vie with you in childish outbursts of pride and egotism. But, you must realize, he won't give you all that money to look at your handsome face. You must be useful.

Julien

And, what is the family like?

Father Pirard

He has two children. A daughter, Mathilde, whose beauty and pride are famous throughout the world, and a son, Count Norbert, who is quite a madman and has an ironic wit feared by all Parisian society.

Julien

Will they despise me?

Father Pirard

They are a very old family. Of course they'll despise

you. If I were you, I'd say very little.

Julien

It seems unlikely I'll be in Paris for very long.

Father Pirard

As you like. But, for a man like you, it's either succeed or be persecuted. There's no middle way for you. I, for example, who am a peaceful, mediocre man, have incurred my share of enemies. You must realize that the tribe of lackeys surrounding the Count will regard you as less than an equal who has unjustly been placed above them. Beneath a show of friendliness, they'll try to make you blunder.

Julien

I defy them to do that.

Father Pirard

You have decided, I see. Go then, and carry this letter to the Bishop. Here is money. Buy yourself some suits. Do not return, but rather, meet me in Paris three days hence. I leave you at liberty. Ruin yourself, if you must. I'll be delivered from my weakness of thinking about you.

Julien

Father, your blessing.

Father Pirard

There. There. Now go. Wait. One more thing. I have the misfortune to be hot tempered; it is possible that you and I may stop seeing each other. Go ahead now. Ruin yourself. Ruin yourself. I was forgetting. Order some extra shirts, cuffs, and boots.

(Julien smiles and goes.)

Father Pirard

If Julien is a frail reed, let him perish. If he is a man of spirit, let him make his way alone.

CURTAIN

ACT II
SCENE 6

A balcony in the Marquis' palace. The balcony opens on a courtyard.

Marquis

People are fond of spaniels. Why should I be ashamed of liking this young ecclesiastic?

Mathilde

It's outrageous to invite this Sorel to your banquet, father.

Marquis

An experiment, Mathilde. Father Pirard maintains that it's wrong to crush the self esteem of those we employ. There's nothing wrong with this man but his unknown face.

Mathilde

Nothing, but his name. Sorel. Besides, he's a bore. He might as well be deaf and dumb for all he ever says.

Marquis

He's discreet.

Mathilde

I rather think he dislikes me.

Marquis

Has he been impolite?

Mathilde

Oh, no. Perfectly correct. I just don't think he cares for the company of women. He thinks we're all silly.

Marquis

So, that's it. My charming daughter has, at last, failed to make a conquest.

Mathilde (furious)

That's not it at all.

Marquis

I respect him for it. You're a bitch at heart, though I'm your father that say it. I can't see how any man could love you, with your haughty ways. I'm glad to see Sorel is a man of sense.

Mathilde

Father, such an expression.

Marquis

Please. We're alone and have no need to worry about the servants. You are the most cold-hearted baggage that ever lived and dared to call herself a woman....

Mathilde

Such talk is unworthy of a diplomat.

Marquis

Hang diplomacy. Candor is one of the few virtues left the aristocracy. You have loved no man.

Mathilde

Except you, papa.

Marquis

Which makes up for everything in my eyes. But really, why don't you behave normally and fall in love?

Mathilde

And, who is there worthy of my love?

Marquis

There are many presentable young men. Surely—

Mathilde

They are either weaklings or fools. I can't abide a man without courage. And I despise courage without intellect and energy.

Marquis

There are many men.

Mathilde

Where? Don't think I haven't looked. All the men of our class are boring. It's disgusting. They're so frightened of another reign of terror they quake in their boots for all their swagger.

Marquis

With good reason. A revolution may not be far off.

Mathilde

In any event, what I want is a man of energy. A bold daredevil.

Marquis

Here comes your brother with Julien.

(Norbert enters from courtyard with Julien.)

Norbert

May I present a young daredevil?

Julien

Count Norbert has been kind enough to take me riding. He was good enough to give me the gentlest horse, but after all, he couldn't tie me to the saddle and I took a couple of spills.

Norbert

One must pay tribute to Julien's courage in riding. It is the only thing about his riding one can praise. (he laughs good naturedly)

Mathilde (giggling)

I'm sorry, I can't help it.

Julien

If it were a question of chopping down wood, I venture to say I'd make a good showing, but riding a horse is something I've done not more than six times in my life.

Marquis

You shall go to riding school. After a few weeks I'll be delighted to ride with you. Now, if you'll excuse me, there's something I must attend to. (he leaves)

Julien

Your father is too kind. Tell me, what must I do to keep from falling off?

Norbert

All sorts of things. For example, sit back in the saddle.

Mathilde

I think he frightens the horse with his gloomy expression.

Norbert

That's unkind.

Mathilde (on the attack)

Your gloomy expression is not in good taste, Mr. Sorel. It's a bored expression that's needed. If you're sad, then there must be something you lack, an admission of inferiority. If you're bored, you're merely hard to please and the thing or person that bored you is inferior. You must realize, my friend, what a mistake you're making.

Julien

I see.

Mathilde

You don't understand the age you live in. Always do the opposite of what people expect of you. That I assure you is the only religion of our time.

Julien

I shall endeavor to be more eccentric.

Mathilde

Ah, but you don't understand. To be eccentric, is to have character. To have character, is to be predictable. You're not an apt pupil, Mr. Sorel.

Norbert

Other provincials who come to Paris admire everything; Julien hates everything. The others have too much affectation, whereas Julien doesn't have enough.

Julien

Well, may I ask Mademoiselle de la Mole whether the mourning she is wearing relates to some personal catastrophe not shared by the rest of the family, or is it an example of her precept that one must always do the opposite of what people expect of you?

Norbert

Touché, Julien. Sister, I think he has the better of you.

Mathilde

But, you really don't know how my custom on this day, Mr. Sorel?

Norbert

I don't think I've ever told him. You see, Julien, on this very day in 1572, our ancestor, Boniface de la Mole, had the honor to be executed for treason. And Marguerite of Navarre, his mistress asked for his head after the execution.

Mathilde

She buried him with her own hands. (Mathilde is enthused) It was the heroic age of France. How I should like to be such a woman. (furious) Norbert, why are you smiling? Don't you see the glory of it?

Norbert

Frankly, I don't. An utterly barbarous story, which, if true, and I doubt it, should be speedily forgotten. I can see you heartily despise me for that sentiment.

Mathilde

Brothers are a real test of a woman's patience, Mr. Sorel. Almost as much as a husband, and a deal harder to be revenged on. Oh, look. There is Monsieur Descoulis crossing the courtyard.

Julien

I've heard of him, but never met him.

Mathilde

What? But, he knows everyone. He's capable of maintaining a lie with each one of his friends, and he has thousands. He's a man who knows how to nourish friendship, how to cuddle it until it grows...and then to suckle it. He's a sort of a sucker up. You must meet him. Monsieur Sorel.

Norbert

I wish you would behave like a lady.

Mathilde

I am one, so why bother? What's the use of taking the trouble to be born a lady if one has to behave like one?

Norbert (trying to change the subject)

From time to time he quarrels with someone and writes seven or eight letters about the subject. Then, he patches it up and writes seven or eight letters overflowing with friendship.

Mathilde

Monsieur Descoulis will be mentioned in history. He brought about the Restoration in company with Monsieur Talleyrand...or so he says.

Norbert

The man is wealthy. I can't understand why he comes here to swallow my father's barbs such as 'How many times have you betrayed your friends, my dear Descoulis? I ask you only because I know you are weak in arithmetic.'

Mathilde

Is it true he betrayed people?

Norbert

Who hasn't these days? He prides himself on being independent.

Mathilde

There's your independent man, bowing almost to the ground to my father.

Norbert

He's lower than if he fell on his knees. My dear Sorel, never, never bow the way that historical personage does. No, not even to God Almighty.

Mathilde

'I'm independent,' he says. 'Why should I have the same opinion today that I had six weeks ago. In that case, my opinion would be my tyrant.' What a fool.

Norbert

Here comes Baron Baton.

Mathilde

I think the servants laugh at him. What a name.

Norbert

Well, it's all in getting used to it. Think how it must have been for the Duc de Bouillon at first. What's in a name? Baton's a good fellow, and I must speak to him before he speaks to my father. You'll excuse me, sister....

(Norbert scampers out.)

Mathilde

He's been gambling again. I know it. (pause during which Julien says not one word) You're not very entertaining, Monsieur.

Julien

I am sorry, Mademoiselle, if my conversation disappoints you. I am, after all, a simple sawyer's son, and not used to all the refinements.

Mathilde

It's not your conversation I complain of, but the lack of it.

Julien

Perhaps I had better go, in that case.

Mathilde

Tell me, sir, do you get that somber face by inheritance, or do you imitate Father Pirard?

Julien

Do you judge people by their faces, then? Allow me to say that Father Pirard's expression results from the fact that his exquisite conscience torments him.

Mathilde

Yes, yes, we all know how good Father Pirard is...but after all, what good is his goodness, if it only makes him gloomy?

Julien

Perhaps, you prefer Monsieur Napier. He has the most cheerful expression, and he is a notorious informer.

Mathilde

Oh, don't be so touchy. (changing the subject) Are you coming to the Ball tonight?

Julien

I'm not aware of being invited.

Mathilde

Of course you are. You're a member of the household.

Julien

It might appear presumptuous, and I am sure I wouldn't want to anyway.

Mathilde

Then come because I want you.

(Mathilde says this with irritation, not because she is imperious, but because he has forced her to ask him. Julien is not aware of this manner, however.)

Julien

So, it seems even during a Ball, I am accountable to every member of the family. God knows whether what I say to you will upset the plans of your father, mother or brother. I have to obey the whim of everyone, like a complete nonentity.

Mathilde

Why do you take it like that?

Julien (icily)

Have no fear, Madame. I will obey your orders.

Mathilde (furious)

See that you do, or I will complain to my father. (she stalks out)

CURTAIN

ACT II
SCENE 7

The Ball. Later the same night.

Two Gentlemen in masks enter.

First Gentleman

Mademoiselle de la Mole acts as though she'd rather die than please anyone who speaks to her.

Second Gentleman

That's the whole secret of being attractive.

First Gentleman

Is that not your opinion, Monsieur Julien?

Julien

Oh, I suppose so. For a parvenu like me, she's worth studying. I must learn what perfection means to your set.

Mathilde

Monsieur Julien—

Julien

Duty calls.

First Gentleman

I'll be damned.

Mathilde

Isn't this the finest Ball of the season?

(Julien remains silent.)

Mathilde (trying again)

I think the quadrille is wonderful, and these ladies dance it beautifully.

Julien

You know yourself, Mademoiselle, I have never been to a Ball before and cannot judge.

(The company is amused.)

Mathilde (determined to be pleased)

How often do you hear such candor in this town? (But,

now that she has come to his rescue from the amusement of others, she cannot forego a shot at him herself) You're a wise man, Monsieur Sorel. You look on all this vanity with the eye of a philosopher, like Rousseau. These follies surprise you, but do not enchant you. Your lofty position permits you to wonder at the follies of mankind.

Julien (stung, but determined to fight back)

In my opinion, Rousseau was a fool to set himself up as a judge of high society; he didn't understand it and he judged with the envy of a man risen above his station. A lackey, pure and simple.

Mathilde

Is the *Social Contract* the work of a lackey?

Julien

Decidedly. He was a parvenu flattered by the company of the nobility and determined to appear superior.

Mathilde

I think it the work of a great man.

Julien

Everyone is entitled to his opinion, Madame, although your principles are a little strange for the daughter of the nation's leading Tory. I shouldn't let your father know of it, considering the fact he disapproves of your reading Walter Scott.

(The company titters.)

(Julien bows and moves off.)

Second Gentleman

He scored off her. Serves the little minx right.

Mathilde (a trifle too loud)

Ah, Norbert, rescue me from this insipid group of people. (the masks are a trifle offended) They all have the most perfect manners, and if it weren't for the boredom they cause, these gentlemen would be very agreeable.

Norbert

Are you being rude again, sister?

Mathilde

Foh. Here comes Monsieur de Croisenois. He wants to marry me. Preserve me, I'll hide. (she ducks down behind her brother)

Norbert

Mathilde, what's gotten into you?

Mathilde

Has he gone?

Norbert

Yes, he's looking for you in the drawing room.

Mathilde

Precisely why I ducked. Smug fool.

Norbert

He's a very distinguished man.

Mathilde

I can't think of anything that distinguishes a man that can't be bought. Maybe a death sentence. Where's Julien?

Norbert

Don't see him.

Mathilde (angry)

He was here a minute ago. Sneak.

Norbert

Why don't you marry de Croisenois, sister? He's got a good name.

Mathilde

He's a conceited fool. What has he ever done? Acquired a fortune. That's considered most meritorious today. Well, let him marry Monsieur Rothschild's daughter. Who is that gentleman?

Norbert

That's Count Altamira.

Mathilde

You mean the man who planned the comic opera revolution in Spain?

Norbert

The same. What a farce it was.

Mathilde

True. Still he acted. I want to meet a real man. Bring him over.

Norbert

I'm not sure a man of his principles is fit company.

Mathilde

Dear brother. You know I cannot bear to be contradicted.

Norbert

But nothing reeks of such bad form as a conspiracy. What could be more unattractive than an unsuccessful conspirator?

Mathilde

Never mind. Go get him.

(Norbert goes to the Count)

Mathilde (to a Gentleman)

A conspirator at a nobleman's ball. How delightful.

Gentleman

It's very strange what this age has come to. Just think, that sleazy Jacobin is the son of Prince Pimental, one of the oldest and noblest families in Naples.

Mathilde (to another Gentleman)

Well, that remark proves that good birth robs a man of his strength of character. Am I doomed to talk nonsense all night?

Norbert (returning)

May I present Count Altamira, sister.

Mathilde

They tell us you're a revolutionary, Count.

Altamira

Nonsense. Nonsense. I merely wish to see the principle of utility applied to governments as it is to economics. What could be more expedient than doing away with kingship and aristocracy?

Mathilde

But, where would civilization be without an aristocracy?

Altamira

No further removed from us than it is at present. Now Bentham has this to say of bicameral government.

Mathilde (between her teeth)

Dear God. (aloud) But, I had taken you to be a sort of Danton. You sound more like a professor. I was hoping to find bloodstains on your shirt.

Altamira

Sorry to disappoint you, Mademoiselle. I launder my shirts quite carefully.

Mathilde

They say you are under some sort of death sentence.

Altamira

I prefer not to be reminded of that. (laughs) Now, as I was saying about Bentham.

Mathilde

Count, will you excuse me, there's someone I simply must see. (she scoots for her life)

(Norbert follows.)

Norbert

Good God, Mathilde, think what you are doing.

Altamira

Never mind, Norbert, there should be some utility in social conventions as well as political. Why stay with someone who's boring you?

Norbert

For the sake of politeness.

Altamira

Nonsense. She did right. She exhibited a noble impatience with the outmoded. We, of the aristocracy, are no longer useful, only ornamental. Soon the only place for us will be on the stage....

Norbert

You must accept my apologies for my sister. I'm going to have a talk with her.

Altamira

Nonsense, nonsense. Why should she want to listen to the ravings of a middle-aged man. She's young.

Julien (has been watching and now approaches)

Count Altamira, I've been looking for you. Would you honor me with a chat? Monsieur de la Mole has asked me to give you this, and I would like to talk of something....

(They go off.)

Norbert

Excuse me, I will attend to my sister.

Gentleman

Today, gentlemen, it is not a man who must be destroyed; it is Paris. Why involve France in something that only concerns Paris? Paris alone with its newspapers has ruined the aristocracy. The modern Babylon must perish.

Norbert (has found Mathilde)

I want to talk to you.

Mathilde

I'm in no humor for it.

Norbert

What's got in to you? Do you want to disgrace our name?

Mathilde

You overestimate my importance. My rudeness is not

about to disgrace the name of a family that has been noble for six hundred years. You're talking like a bourgeois, brother.

Norbert

It was inexcusable.

Mathilde

Oh, I had a headache.

Norbert

Even a parvenu like Julien wouldn't act like this.

Mathilde

Of course not. He wouldn't dare. Anyway, he's so strange and touchy.

(Altamira and Julien have moved near to Mathilde and Norbert.)

Altamira

Yes, Danton was a man.

Mathilde

Good heavens, can the Count be another Danton? He has such a noble face and Danton was so horribly ugly.

Norbert

I see you aren't about to listen. Well, I don't have to witness the disgrace you'll bring on us. Good night.

(Mathilde, alone now, eavesdrops on Julien and Altamira.)

Mathilde (to herself)

I'm certainly very bored tonight. (to Julien) Wasn't Danton a butcher?

Julien

In the eyes of certain prejudiced classes. Actually, he began his career like a number of others I see here tonight...as a lawyer.

Mathilde

You are satiric, I see.

Julien

He also had an enormous advantage with women because he was extraordinarily ugly.

Mathilde

That's an original thought. Not too flattering to the ladies.

Altamira

Look at that man, the Prince d'Araceli, the Spanish Ambassador. This morning, he formally asked for my extradition. Tonight, he drank my health. If I'm returned to Spain, there's no doubt I'll hang.

Julien

The bastard.

Altamira

I spoke of myself only to provide a vivid example. I understand his point of view. Only doing his job, nothing personal. No reason not to drink your health. Look at him, he can't keep his eyes off his Star of Malta for five minutes. A hundred years ago the Star was a real honor, beyond the reach of a man like that. Today, only men like that want it. He'd have a whole town hanged to get it.

Julien

Is that the price he paid for it?

Altamira

No. Thirty rich liberals sufficed. What a monster!

Julien

A man like that doesn't deserve to live.

(Mathilde is practically letting her hair rest on Julien's shoulder, so interested has she become in the conversation.)

Altamira

As you said, you don't have to do much these days to get it. Had he murdered a whole town, that, at least, would have been noteworthy.

Julien

Infamous.

Altamira

You're very young. My sister is kind and gentle. In 1815 I was hiding in her house. The day she heard of Marshall Ney's execution, she began to clap her hands and dance.

Julien

That's hard to believe.

Altamira

That's partisanship. There are no passions left in this century. That's why people are so bored. The cruelest acts committed in the most inoffensive ways, without any cruelty intended.

Julien

So much the worse. When people commit crimes they should at least take pleasure in committing them.... What other justification is there?

Altamira

You're right. And, most people forget their crimes these days. They're so accustomed to them and bored by them. And so does the world. Whereas, I am considered a Jacobin monster.

Mathilde

Perfectly true.

(Altamira is astonished by her remark. Julien doesn't deign giving her a glance.)

Altamira

I might add, that my revolution was unsuccessful only because I was unwilling to rearrange the anatomy of a half dozen men.

Julien (eyes blazing)

At that time, you didn't know the rules of the game. Now....

Altamira

I knew the rules, Julien. I preferred to play by my own rules.

Julien

But, the end justifies the means. If, instead of being a nonentity, I had a certain amount of power, I'd be willing to hang three men to save four.

(Mathilde's and Julien's eyes lock for an instant, then she withdraws angrily.)

Mathilde (asserting her superiority)

Would you get me an ice, Monsieur Sorel? I'm thirsty. (her eyes say 'dare to refuse')

Julien (equally defiant)

How can I refuse the daughter of the man who employs me?

Mathilde

What a magnificent ball, Count. There's nothing

lacking.

Altamira

Thought is lacking.

Mathilde

You're here, Count. Doesn't that make thought present, also?

Altamira

I'm here because of my name. It's about five centuries older vintage than anyone else here...except yours, my noble hostess. But thought is hated here...and throughout the country. What other race always starts profound conversations and stops them before anything intelligent is said?

Mathilde

That's because our society values decorum above all things.

Altamira

Well, I'm happy to be in the company of a woman whose conduct to me has proved she does not. You'll excuse me, Mademoiselle. (he bows and goes off)

(Mathilde is furious, but cannot think of a retort.

Besides, she knows she deserves it. Julien returns with a glass for her.)

Mathilde

Thank you. You could have brought one for yourself. I'll toast you.

Julien

I'm sorry. I wasn't sure it was permitted. I didn't wish to be presumptuous.

(Julien has succeeded in making her feel that her superior position in society is a distinct disadvantage. Mathilde ignores his remark and tries again.)

Mathilde

You're obviously thinking about something very interesting, Monsieur Sorel. Can it be some curious anecdote about the conspiracy that sent Count Altamira here to us?

Julien

On the contrary, my mind's a blank.

Mathilde

Tell me what you're thinking about. I'm dying to know. I give you my word, I'll be discreet. (lightly)

What can have made you abandon your usual coldness and become an inspired creature like one of Michelangelo's prophets?

Julien (seriously)

Well...I'm wondering, should a man who wants to drive crime and ignorance from this earth, pass over it like a whirlwind and do evil indiscriminately?

Mathilde (vaguely frightened)

You talk wildly.

Julien

You needn't be afraid. I'm of no account. As a matter of fact, if your friend the Count had compromised a few people with crimes, they wouldn't have been swept aside so easily. They were only presumptuous, chattering children...like me. But, by what right do I judge them? After all, they actually dared to attempt something....

Mathilde

You are quite sincere. You are made unhappy by your extraordinary ambition. You need a woman to love you. But, I see no love in you. You are so cold.

Julien

What kind of woman would you suggest for such a man?

Mathilde

A woman who is bored with her life and in search of adventure. Of necessity, such a woman must be an aristocrat. And, since your ambition is great, you had best seek out a woman whose boredom has reached the highest pitch. No doubt, you will find her in the highest ranks of the aristocracy.

Julien

You are very witty.

Mathilde

In fact, I can't suggest a better woman for you than... myself, Monsieur.

Julien (coolly)

I think you are making fun of me.

Mathilde (smiling)

Perhaps. Perhaps not.

Marquis de la Mole (coming up)

Ah, Julien. We are going to put that famous memory of yours to work. At ten o'clock, come to my study. There I will entrust you with a mission. You'll ride at dawn for Strasbourg.

Julien

Yes, sir. I will not fail you.

Marquis

If I thought you were capable of failure, I would not trust you. Take some pistols, it may be dangerous. Ten o'clock, now.

Julien

Ten o'clock.

(The Marquis leaves hurriedly.)

Mathilde

What did you think of my suggestion?

Julien

It seems I am about to have an adventure.

Mathilde

Is that the way you look at it?

Julien

I beg your pardon, Mademoiselle. I didn't hear you. What did you say?

Mathilde

Insupportable!

Julien

I'm truly sorry, Mademoiselle, but I was caught up with the thought of riding to Strasbourg at dawn.

Mathilde

You may be in great danger.

Julien

It will be good to run some hazards again. I haven't for a long time.

Mathilde

Back in the days of Boniface de la Mole, life was a series of adventures. Nowadays, an efficient police system has eliminated that. The unexpected has vanished. If it crops up in someone else's ideas, it's overwhelmed with epigrams.

Julien

Yes...even for a man of action.

Mathilde

The best a woman can hope for is a love affair. A grand passion. That kind of amusement has many dangers. (thoughtfully) So much the better! Well? Have you nothing to say to me?

Julien

You were speaking generally, I took it.

Mathilde

Are you making fun of me? I'm patient, sir, but I won't be much longer.

Julien

I can't imagine what you want me to say, or what I've done to offend you. Allow me to apologize and withdraw. It's almost time to go to your father.

Mathilde

You're going to make me say it, aren't you? Oh, you

heartless tyrant. What kind of monster have I allowed myself to love?

Julien

I don't understand.

Mathilde

You understand very well, indeed. You're going away and I must speak. Oh, you beast. With your character, you shouldn't be shy in telling me you love me.

Julien

No doubt, you speak to ridicule my simplicity.

Mathilde

Haven't you triumphed over me enough? Directly you leave my father, come to my apartment. I will not let you go without loving you.

Julien

But, I leave at dawn.

Mathilde

So much more enchanted will be our love. Each moment will be precious.

Julien

But, how will I get in without being seen?

Mathilde

You will take the ladder in the garden and climb up the balcony.

Julien

That's risky, isn't it?

Mathilde

The man who loves me must take risks.

Julien

But, I just can't leave it standing there at your window all night.

Mathilde

Lower it with some rope. I always have some rope in my room.

(A look of perfect comprehension comes over Julien's face.)

Julien (ironic)

So, I'm favored over Monsieur de Croisenois. How is it possible that a poor tutor like me could prevail over his handsome mustaches?

Mathilde

I know you have a manly heart. Don't give him a thought. He means nothing to me. I want to test your courage, I admit it.

Julien (ironic)

And, when I come to your apartment, you will grant me a happiness which will place me above all other men?

Mathilde

So, you act like my master already! (she flounces and looks furiously at him) But, I must speak to you. (icily) It's an accepted convention: one speaks to one's lover. (frigidly) I have promised you and decided if you show supreme courage, I must make you happy. I KEEP MY WORD! Otherwise, I'd be the one lacking in character. I shall do my duty.

Julien (equally cold)

I will not be behindhand in the duty I owe myself.

Mathilde (mocking)

Of course, I may be mistaken in you. Perhaps you only have the appearance of a superior man.

Julien

I shall not refuse such a pleasure. I'm not that stupid. Your love makes me the equal of all men in this room. I shall keep my appointment without fail. Now, (he bows) you must excuse me. I must go to your father.

Mathilde (as he leaves)

Our ecstasy seems a little forced. Passion seems to be a model we are imitating rather than feeling. But, it would be immoral for me to retreat now. Can I have been mistaken? Is it possible I don't love him? And, my God, what's worse, he hasn't even said he loves me.

The Reactionary Gentleman (passing by in conversation with another)

Form your battalions. Will you go on talking without acting? In fifty years there will be nothing in Europe but Presidents and Republics...not a single king. And without those letters K-I-N-G, the priests and the noblemen will also disappear. I see only CANDIDATES currying favor with unwashed majorities.

CURTAIN

ACT III
SCENE 8

The balcony.

Mathilde enters, followed by Julien.

Mathilde

So, Monsieur, apparently you think you've acquired some very strong rights over me. In spite of my clearly expressed wishes, you insist on speaking to me. Do you realize that no one else has ever dared so much?

Julien

Don't you love me anymore?

Mathilde

Actually, my passion for you, poor boy, lasted only from midnight when you came up the ladder with pistols in belt, until Mass. I saw clearly that you thought you had acquired a master's rights. From that moment, my passion began to cool.

Julien

You are very proud.

Mathilde

And, if it weren't for the fact I think your vanity capable of revealing the nature of our relationship, I'd break it off, here and now.

Julien (controlling himself)

Have no fear. I swear that I'll never reveal your secret. In fact, I'd never speak to you again, if it were not for the fact that your reputation might suffer from so noticeable a change.

Mathilde (flatly)

Then, it is over.

Julien (calmly)

It's over. Do not think that I am ungrateful. You conferred a great honor on me...though I clearly understand it proceeded more from your notions of romance than from any worth on my part. I must admit that I was born with a very unimaginative and unfortunate character.

Mathilde

So, that is what you are like! And I've given myself to you. The first man who came along.

Julien (furious)

The first? (he picks up a letter opener from the table)

Mathilde (crying)

Are you going to kill me?

Julien

That would be altogether too melodramatic. (he replaces the letter opener) More appropriate in a comedy than in our relationship.

Mathilde (interested) Were you really going to kill me?

(Julien makes no reply.)

Mathilde

What will you do now?

Julien (coolly)

Why, I think I shall endeavor to forget you.

Mathilde (furious)

How will you ever do that? You, a little nobody? Why you'll boast of it forever.

Julien

Please notice that you are speaking loudly. You'll be heard in the next room.

Mathilde

What does that matter? Who will dare to tell me I've been overhead? I want to cure your petty self-esteem forever of any silly ideas you may have conceived about me.

Julien

I made the great mistake of treating you AS IF I loved you...and you believing it, despise me. What it is to have the advantage of an aristocratic education!

Mathilde

So. It was reserved for me, the daughter of the noblest house of France to see my most indecent advances scorned. And scorned by whom? By one of my father's servants.

Julien

Say what you please. The disgrace, if any, is yours, not mine. I can't help my humble birth. But you might have conducted yourself in accordance with the laws of honor. Now, if you will excuse me, I must write a letter.

(Julien seats himself at a table and begins to write.)

Mathilde

Who are you writing to?

Julien

That's no concern of yours.

Mathilde

You are writing to another woman!

Julien

You have no right to question me about that any longer.

Mathilde

Who is it? I won't have you go from me to a servant.

Julien

Put yourself at ease, she is a woman of honor.

Mathilde

This is something I can't tolerate. You're forgetting me completely. Me, your wife! Your conduct to me is horrible, Monsieur.

Julien

Ah, so now you call yourself my wife. The proud Mademoiselle de la Mole is now the humble Madame Sorel. But, I note, Madame, though you honor me, it is an honor that I have not solicited.

Mathilde

You can treat me like that? You know I love you. (she throws herself into his arms) Punish me for my unspeakable pride. You're my master; I'm your slave. Forgive me for trying to rebel. If you like I'll go to my knees.

Julien

Someone might disturb us. We'll postpone that till later.

Mathilde

I must show you now. (she takes the letter opener and cuts off a lock of hair) This is given you by your servant as a token of eternal obedience. If ever I am led astray by my detestable pride, point to my hair and say it's not a question of love, it's a question of duty.

Julien (overjoyed)

Mathilde, if only you knew how little I've enjoyed this triumph, and how much it cost me not to.... (he catches himself and stops)

Mathilde

What's the matter, my darling?

Julien

I'm lying, and I'm lying to you. I reproach myself for it. God knows, I respect you too much to lie to you. You love me, you're devoted to me; I have no need to make set speeches to you.

Mathilde

Good Heavens! All those wonderful things you've been saying...nothing but set speeches?

Julien

Yes. I invented them for a woman who bored me. Forgive me.

(Mathilde starts to cry.)

Julien

My detestable memory offers me resources, and I misuse them.

Mathilde (breathing hard)

That set speech. It was for the woman you were writing to?

Julien

I confess it.

Mathilde

Let me see the letter.

Julien

No.

Mathilde

Has she made you the same sacrifice that I have?

Julien

That is a question a man of honor cannot answer.

Mathilde (rushing to the table and opening the drawer)

Madame de Fervaques. Let us see if you have any letters from her. (she stares) My God. Here are a dozen letters all addressed to her...and not yet sent.

Julien

I plan my campaign in advance.

Mathilde

You despise her. You, a little nobody, despise one of the greatest ladies in France.

Julien

I knew you would start pulling rank again.

Mathilde

Do you love her?

Julien

Gratitude alone would be enough to attach me to her. She has consoled me when I was despised.

Mathilde

Oh!

Julien

And your feelings are not to be trusted. The moment you feel I love you as much as you love me, you start to despise me.

Mathilde

I will give you any guarantee that you like.

Julien

You just promised to be my slave, and within two minutes, you assume the tone of a master.

Mathilde

Say what you want.

Julien

What guarantee will you give me that your love will last two days?

Mathilde

The intensity of my love, and my unhappiness, if you no longer love me.

Julien

That's not enough.

Mathilde

I've offended you. You've a right to be angry with me. You want guarantees, my darling...that's only fair. Elope with me. We'll go to London. I'll be ruined forever. (this is not easy for her) All right, dishonor me. That's a guarantee, isn't it?

Julien

And, how do I know, once you're dishonored, to use your expression...my presence won't be unwelcome to you? I'm not a monster. I don't wish to ruin your reputation. It's not your position in society that's the obstacle, it's your character. One sign of affection from me and you're ready to throw me over.

Mathilde (after a pause)

I hadn't intended to tell you this. And, I've been so upset, I'd almost forgotten. I shall give you a guarantee you cannot doubt. You are to be the father of my child. Do you doubt me now? I'm your wife, forever.

Julien

Good God! And you were going to break with me

anyway? (Mathilde nods mutely) You were going to deprive me of my child? Well, then, what were you gong to do?

Mathilde (crying)

I really hadn't thought about it. (childishly) To tell the truth, I was more afraid of your finding out how much I love you. I didn't want to be your slave. (she sobs)

Julien

Why must you be a master or a slave. Couldn't you be an equal? Is it so hard?

Mathilde

What are we going to do? I can't hide it more than another month.

Julien

Well, I won't let my child be murdered. I won't have it...do you hear?

Mathilde

Who said anything about that? Do you think I'd give up our child?

Julien

Then, what will you do?

Mathilde

I'm going to write to my father.

Julien

Are you mad?

Mathilde

He's more than a father to me: he's a friend. I think it would be unworthy of both of us to try to deceive him...even for a moment. In fact, I'll tell him now.

Julien

What are you going to do?

Mathilde (proudly)

My duty!

Julien

But, he'll drive me out of the house in disgrace.

Mathilde

That's his right, and we must respect it. I'll give you

my arm, and we'll walk out the front door together, in broad daylight.

Julien

Wait a while, anyway.

Mathilde

I can't. My duty is clear.

Julien

Then, I order you to wait. Your honor is safe. I'm your husband. That step is momentous; we must think it through.

Mathilde (scornful)

You mean to say 'think of what he may do.'

Julien

I pity him. He has been my benefactor, but I do not fear him. I owe him considerable gratitude. He procured this medal for me.

Mathilde

It's going to come out, Julien. It's got to. And, it's better we are frank. (she pulls a bell cord and a servant appears) Ask my father to step in here, please.

(The servant bows and goes out.)

Mathilde

Be sure that whatever happens, I will stand by you.

Marquis (entering)

Is something wrong, dear? You look so solemn.

Mathilde

I dread some things I must say to you. I fear you will be upset.

Marquis

What can you have done to upset me? After all, I'm your father.

Mathilde

I shall cry, when I think of the pain I shall cause you.

Marquis

There, there. I know you love me more than anyone.

Mathilde

After my husband, you are, and always will be, the dearest person in all the world to me.

Marquis

What are your talking about? You haven't married without my consent, have you?

Mathilde

Not exactly.

Marquis

Julien, you're a sensible person. Maybe you can make some sense out of this. She's married, but not exactly?

(Julien shrugs.)

Mathilde

I'm pregnant, father.

Marquis

Well, who is it? De Croisenois! Well, it can easily be managed. But, why do you tell me in front of Monsieur Sorel?

Mathilde

I shall not be a duchess, father. If your affection for me will grant me a small allowance, I will live anywhere you say, Switzerland for example, with my husband.

His name is so obscure that no one will recognize your daughter in Madame Sorel.

Marquis (stunned)

Are you telling me, that you've allowed yourself to be indiscreet with a sawyer's son?

Mathilde

I'm telling you, so that it can be kept from becoming public. So that you will have time to act.

Marquis (to Julien)

You vile little seducer.

Mathilde

He is not. I loved him first. It was I who seduced him. As for his being a sawyer's son...I have inherited too noble a heart from you to place my affections on anyone who is vulgar.

Marquis

Aren't there hundreds of men of your own class with whom you could fall in love, if you had to.... Haven't I surrounded you with them?

Mathilde

Yes, and you put true merit before my eyes, too. Why did you do it, then...to torment me? if you did not want me to love? Have not you, yourself, praised him above all others?

Marquis

My head is spinning.

Mathilde

Why do you pretend to respect these nobles more than Julien? They are afraid of everything...they are persons of second class. All they aspire to is my fortune. How very heroic! Between Julien and me there is no contract, no middle-class ceremony... everything is heroic. It's like the love of Marguerite of Valois for Boniface de la Mole.

Marquis

This comes from your romantic notions. Oh, that I ever let you read a history book.

Mathilde

Is it my fault that men of my class are frightened even of ridicule? My Julien likes to act alone. He despises others, and that is why I don't despise him. I am a weak woman, but at least I wasn't led astray by his looks like a school girl. It wasn't his looks that seduced me, but his mind, his talk of revolution.

Marquis

Revolution. What next!

Mathilde

If there's a revolution, why shouldn't Julien be another Danton. Why shouldn't I be a Madame Roland?

Marquis

A Danton! Why not a Robespierre? I'm sure he's capable of having us all guillotined. My daughter and a Robespierre. (quietly) You're mad.

Mathilde

An ordinary girl would have sought her man among the social butterflies that pass for men. As Julien's companion, I'll continually attract attention. Instead of living in fear of revolution...like our cousins, who are afraid even to scold their servants...I'll play a leading part in it.

Marquis

Oh, you want to be a revolutionary, too?

Mathilde

What does he lack? Money? I'll give it to him. I've already shown great boldness by daring to fall in love with him, a man beneath my station. You think I'm a fool. But, I'd be a fool to marry de Croisenois. What good is a love that makes you yawn? I might as well become pious.

Marquis

So, you want to marry this little Robespierre?

Mathilde

Yes, yes, yes, yes. Suppose there is another revolution. What part will de Croisenois and my brother play? It's written in advance; sublime resignation. They'd let themselves be slaughtered, without a word. It would be bad form to fight. My little Julien would shoot the Jacobin who came to arrest him, if he had the slightest hope of escaping. He's not afraid of showing bad form.

Marquis

No, that he's not. If only he could die by some accident, we could still arrange....

Mathilde

If he's dead, I'll die, too. It's you who'll be the cause of my death. But, I swear to you, I'll go into mourning for him and publicly make myself known as his widow. I'll send out funeral cards. You can count on it. You know my character.

Marquis

Can't you see, he's nothing but a little adventurer. And, I trusted him.

Mathilde

And rightly so. He has always been loyal. You've always said so.

Marquis

Only in appearance. He's planned this all along. He's after our money, or perhaps, worse. He seeks to ruin us from spite. I'll never let you marry him.

Mathilde

That's nonsense.

Marquis

I wouldn't have believed it myself, if I hadn't received this letter barely an hour ago.

Julien

What letter?

Marquis

It's from Madame de Reynal, whose children you tutored. It reads: 'Dear Marquis, I must warn you of a young man you have placed great trust in. Formerly, as you know, he was employed in this household. I fear it is his habit to seduce the women of the house. I have been brought by religion to confess my shame.'

Mathilde

I know all about that. It's not what you think.

Marquis

It's exactly what I think. How can you be so blind? I prefer you to bear a bastard. I will never permit you to marry him.

Julien (strangled)

I have been betrayed. (he picks up the letter opener and runs out)

Mathilde

Julien, what are you going to do? Let me go after him.

Julien! What are you going to do?

(The Marquis prevents her from following him, as the Curtain drops.)

CURTAIN

ACT III
SCENE 9

Julien's cell; an hour before dawn.

Fouqué

That stupid jury.

Julien

The crime was premeditated. I stabbed Madame de Reynal in cold blood.

Fouqué

Yes, but you didn't have to stir up the jury against you.

Julien

Why shouldn't I tell them what I think of them? Every one of them a bourgeois. 'Gentlemen of the Jury, I have no mercy for you. I have no illusions: death is awaiting me and it will be just. I am guilty of attempting to kill a lady worthy of the highest respect. Madame de Reynal had been like a mother to me. My crime was atrocious, it was premeditated. I, therefore, deserve death. But, even if I were innocent, I see men among you who want to punish me and discourage forever men of my class who have had the boldness to mingle with you. That is my crime, gentlemen. In this jury, I do not see a single peasant who has grown rich by his own efforts. I see only members of the middle class whom I have outraged.'

Fouqué

But, don't you see, they hadn't even thought of their class interest until you called it to their attention? They were sympathetic. People knew you were her lover. They thought you were jealous.

Julien

And, was I to let them think that? Let me go on living in my dreams. A man dies as best he can. My relations with other people will soon be cut short. It's enough I have to be degraded standing before them. I don't have to respect them. I don't have to perform for them.

Fouqué

Why won't you agree at least to Mathilde's plan to bribe the guard and escape? And, for God's sake, why don't you sign your appeal? Even now, if you sign the appeal, the execution will be delayed. It's irregular, but with Mademoiselle de la Mole's money....

Julien

What is the point of living another six weeks, at most? At any rate, I consider myself rightly condemned to death. I tried to kill the only woman I ever loved, out of ambition.

Fouqué

So, it's remorse.

Julien

I abandoned Louise for a woman that...no, that's not true, either. I don't hate Mathilde; but I don't love her. I was in the grip of a strange passion. It seems I have not been true to either of the two women who love me. And, they are the only ones who ever did. Do you know, my father hated me? We did each other as much harm as we could. He came here last night, and the only way I could think to get rid of him was to tell him I'd left him some money in my will. You should have seen how he changed. He'd been cursing me for disgracing the family. Suddenly, he was entirely reconciled to me.

Fouqué

How horrible. How unnatural.

Julien

Horrible, yes, but not unnatural. There's nothing that's natural except the strength of a lion. My father, despite his avarice, is a strong man. He's worth a hundred of those sniveling idiots on the jury. Someday he'll show people his gold and say, 'At this price, which of you wouldn't be delighted to have his son guillotined?'

Fouqué

Julien, don't think like that.

Julien

And I applaud him for it. I applaud him for having the courage to know what he is. I have always loved truth, and hypocrisy is everywhere. He's honest, anyway. That's something. If only there were a true religion...perhaps in a true Christianity where the priests are paid no more than the Apostles. But, that's nonsense...Saint Paul was paid with the pleasure of commanding, talking, and making others listen. What a fool I am! I see a gothic Cathedral with ancient stained glass windows and my heart imagines the priest who goes with those windows.

My soul would understand him. My soul needs him. But, what do I find? A conceited fool with dirty hair!

Fouqué

Julien, you shouldn't talk about the Church like that.

Julien

Why not? Who better than I? I've lived around priests all my life!

Fouqué

What about Father Pirard?

Julien

A very worthy man. But he's a stoic, not a Christian. And he's better than any of them. How is it possible to believe in a God that is served by such men?

Fouqué

Calm down, Julien, I beg you.

Julien

And which God, anyway? Certainly not the God of the Bible. Better to live and die in isolation....

Fouqué

What are you saying, Julien?

Julien

Haven't I always lived in isolation? Ah, but it's unjust. I cursed their hypocrisy. But, all my life I've only studied to go them one better. My life has been one long hypocrisy. I'm depressed.

Fouqué

Most men are at such a time.

Julien

It's not death that's depressing. I have nothing to live for now. If only I hadn't been a fool. If only I'd had sense and had five more years of life to live with Louise. It's amazing I thought I wanted to kill her over that letter. Now, I'd like nothing better than to live with her on a few hundred francs a year in some little village like Verge.

Fouqué

So, you loved her more than this aristocratic girl?

Julien

Yes, but you must promise me not to tell Mathilde what

I have told you. Mathilde is a queen and I owe her much. She loves me, and I respect her. She made a great sacrifice of pride in choosing a beggar like me. In fact, it's the greatest compliment anyone has ever paid me. She is my wife, but not the mistress of my heart.

Fouqué

That must be your wife I hear now. I'll wait outside.

(Fouqué leaves.)

Julien

The trouble with being in prison is that you can't refuse visitors.

Mathilde (entering, running to his arms)

That infamous lawyer betrayed me. He promised he would bribe your guard, but he lied and pocketed the money.

Julien

Well, well, it will all be over soon. (reciting)

'By virtue of the right That a steadfast heart imbued with vast designs Has o'er the cruder minds of common men....' (talking) It's really amusing. Since I've been doomed to die, all the poetry I've ever learned in my life has been coming back to me. It must be a sign of decay.

Mathilde

Oh, Julien, don't despair.

Julien

Despair. Why should I? Wasn't I admirable the other day before the jury? I was improvising...for the first and last time in my life. I lack the advantage of your noble birth, but your lofty soul has raised me to your level. Do you think that Boniface de la Mole behaved any better before his judges, hey?

Mathilde

What do I care about Boniface de la Mole? I want to get you out of here!

Julien

I'm afraid that won't work. No one knows the source of the Nile, and no one will ever see Julien Sorel weak. Because he isn't weak.

Mathilde

Will you stop this ridiculous posturing and listen to me? We're not done for yet. I've a new lawyer. He's waiting outside.

Julien

Dear girl, this is the last time I shall feel that noble heart of yours....

Mathilde

Will you listen to me? He's waiting outside.

Julien

Who's waiting?

Mathilde

The lawyer. There's still time to sign your appeal. It's late, but they'll predate it. It's all agreed.

Julien

I won't appeal.

Mathilde

What? Would you please tell me why not!

Julien

Because, now I feel I am ready to die without giving others too much cause for laughter. Who knows whether I'd be in such good condition two months from now. Moreover, I foresee visits from priests.

What could be more distasteful?

Mathilde

What right have you to die, unless I give you permission?

Julien (smiling)

Mathilde, Mathilde, Heaven owed it to the glory of your lineage to let you be born a man. Look, in a few short minutes I'll fight a duel with a character who's noted for his coolness and remarkable skill. Very remarkable. He's never missed once.

Mathilde

What is wrong with you? Where is your ambition? Your will? Oh, can I have been wrong about you? Are you a coward?

(Mathilde bursts into tears.)

Julien

You know better. But what can I hope for, even if I escape? I am a common murderer and my name will follow me everywhere. You say my ambition is gone. Indeed, it has. For what more can I do than live? And, if I can do no more than live, what's the use of living? You see that, Mathilde? You must see that?

Mathilde

You're so cruel. What about me? What about the baby?

Julien

You will marry Monsieur de Croisenois, or someone like him.

Mathilde

What, after I've been dishonored?

Julien

Dishonor cannot stain a name like yours. You'll be a widow, and the widow of a madman, that's all. It won't stand in your way. You'll make a brilliant career.

Mathilde

If you die, I'll die with you. What would people say if I didn't? They'll compare us to Romeo and Juliet. To Marguerite of Valois and Boniface de la Mole.

Julien

I forbid you to take your own life. You must take care of our child. Do you hear? Promise me.

Mathilde

You are very cruel. Very well, I promise.

Julien

Good. Fifteen years from now, you'll regard the love you once felt for me as an excusable folly. But, a folly all the same.

Mathilde

Are you trying to torment me? How can you think things like that, let alone say them?

Julien

Perhaps one day, they'll abolish the death penalty. Then my memory won't be so infamous. I'll die. I deserve death.

Mathilde

How can you feel remorse for that woman? It was a noble vengeance.

Julien

I loved her once. Ah, Mathilde, you'll make a handsome widow.

Mathilde

A widow who will not be given to much gaiety, I am afraid. For she has lived to see that her husband no longer loves her.

Julien

What?

Mathilde

You love her. I see it now. That's why you've given up. (she starts to cry again)

(The cell door opens. Fouqué, a Jailer, and a Priest enter.)

Fouqué

It's time, Julien.

Priest

Repent, my son...think of the good your repentance will do. Think of the example.

Julien

Get that fellow away from me.

Priest

Think of the effect of your spectacular conversion.

Julien

And, what will I have left, if I despise myself? I was ambitious; I don't regret it. I acted in accordance with the standards of my time. Come, sir. (to the Jailer) My soul is ready.

Jailer

So is la Guillotine. Do you want a Mask?

Julien

That will be unnecessary.

(Mathilde runs to kiss him.)

Julien (breaking past)

See to her, Fouqué.

(Julien exits with the Jailer and the Priest, who has not given up.)

Mathilde

I want to see it.

Fouqué

Are you sure it's wise?

Mathilde

I am not about to argue with you.

Fouqué

We can watch from the cell window.

(They stand watching.)

Fouqué

Now, he is on the scaffold.

(A thud.)

Fouqué

And now?

Mathilde

With God.

CURTAIN

ABOUT THE AUTHOR

Frank J. Morlock has written and translated many plays since retiring from the legal profession in 1992. His translations have also appeared on Project Gutenberg, the Alexandre Dumas Père web page, Literature in the Age of Napoléon, Infinite Artistries.com, and Munsey's (formerly Blackmask). In 2006 he received an award from the North American Jules Verne Society for his translations of Verne's plays. He lives and works in México.

www.ingramcontent.com/pod-product-compliance
Lightning Source LLC
LaVergne TN
LVHW041626070426
835507LV00008B/478